The Best Pet for Me

Is a HAMSTER a Good Pet for Me?

Jason Brainard

PowerKiDS press

New York

Published in 2020 by The Rosen Publishing Group, Inc.
29 East 21st Street, New York, NY 10010

First Edition

Editor: Elizabeth Krajnik
Book Design: Rachel Rising

Photo Credits: Cover, p. 1 Olena Kurashova/Shutterstock.com; Cover, pp.1,3, 4, 6, 8, 10 ,12, 14, 16, 18, 20, 22, 23, 24 (background) Anna_leni/Shutterstock.com; Back cover, p. 3 Igor Kovalchuk/Shutterstock.com; p. 4 Eric Isselee/Shutterstock.com; pp. 5, 11, 18 stock_shot/Shutterstock.com; p. 7 PHOTOSTOCK-ISRAEL/Science Photo Library/Getty Images; p. 8 Happy monkey/Shutterstock.com; p. 9 Kristina Stasiuliene/Shutterstock.com; p. 12 Coprid/Shutterstock.com; p. 13 polya_olya/Shutterstock.com; p. 14 HelloRF Zcool/Shutterstock.com; p. 15 fantom_rd/Shutterstock.com; p. 16 Africa Studio/Shutterstock.com; p. 17 Victoria Rak/Shutterstock.com; p. 19 AtiwatPhotography/Shutterstock.com; p. 20 Natalia7/Shutterstock.com; p. 21 W Tammanoon/Shutterstock.com; p. 22 Tsekhmister/Shutterstock.com.

Library of Congress Cataloging-in-Publication Data

Names: Brainard, Jason, author.
Title: Is a hamster a good pet for me? / Jason Brainard.
Description: New York : PowerKids Press, [2020] | Series: The best pet for me | Includes index.
Identifiers: LCCN 2018051644| ISBN 9781725301122 (paperback) | ISBN 9781725301146 (library bound) | ISBN 9781725301139 (6 pack)
Subjects: LCSH: Hamsters as pets–Juvenile literature.
Classification: LCC SF459.H3 B728 2020 | DDC 636.935/6–dc23
LC record available at https://lccn.loc.gov/2018051644

Manufactured in the United States of America

CPSIA Compliance Information: Batch #CSPK19. For Further Information contact Rosen Publishing, New York, New York at 1-800-237-9932.

Contents

A Cute Pet

Have you ever wanted to get a pet? Pets can be fun and cuddly. A pet may even become another member of the family. However, owning a pet is a big **responsibility**. If you think you're ready for a pet, you'll have to think about what kind you want.

Many people have larger pets such as cats and dogs. However, smaller animals such as hamsters can be good pets, too. Hamsters are cute, fluffy, and active. Even though they don't take up much space, they still need lots of care and attention. Read on to see if a hamster is a good pet for you.

Pet Report

A hamster is a kind of rodent that has short legs, a round body, a short tail, and large cheek pouches. Other rodents kept as pets include mice, rats, gerbils, guinea pigs, and chinchillas.

The most common species, or kind, of hamster kept as a pet is *Mesocricetus auratus*, which is also called the golden hamster or the Syrian hamster.

The History of Hamsters

Hamsters haven't always been people's pets. Hamsters have existed on Earth for millions of years. **Fossils** of **extinct** hamster species from 16.4 million years ago have been found in Europe and North Africa. Today, there are about 20 species of wild hamsters that live in parts of Europe, Asia, and the Middle East.

The Syrian hamster comes from the area surrounding Aleppo, Syria. In 1797, a doctor named Alexander Russell found them in the wild. About 40 years later, the species was officially named the golden hamster. Today, these hamsters come in a number of colors and are more often called Syrian hamsters.

Pet Report

In 1930, zoologist Israel Aharoni led an expedition to find golden hamsters in Aleppo. He found a golden hamster and her 11 young in a nest 8 feet (2.4 m) underground.

Of the 12 golden hamsters taken from Aleppo in 1930, only four survived and had babies of their own. It's unknown how many Syrian hamsters exist in the wild today.

Hamster Basics

Different kinds of hamsters are different sizes. An adult Syrian hamster weighs more than 3.5 ounces (100 g) and is about 7.1 inches (18 cm) long. Female Syrian hamsters are usually larger than males.

Female Syrian hamsters can have babies while they're quite young. A hamster is pregnant for 16 to 19 days and can have up to five litters per year. Each litter usually has six to eight babies, but there can be as many as 16. The babies are born blind and hairless and weigh about 0.07 to 0.11 ounce (2 to 3 g).

Pet Syrian hamsters are fully grown when they're about two months old. They usually live to be two to three years old.

A Hamster's Life

Most hamsters, especially Syrian hamsters, are solitary, which means they like to be alone. They're nocturnal, which means they are active at night and sleep during the day. They may also be active in the early morning or late evening.

Hamsters are great diggers and make **burrows** that have one or two entrances. These burrows have different rooms for different purposes, such as nesting and food storage. Hamsters also use tunnels made by other animals.

Hamsters eat grains, fruit, the green parts of plants, and sometimes other small animals. They carry food in their cheek pouches back to their burrow for storage.

Pet Report

Even though hamsters don't **hibernate**, some go through periods of torpor. This is a state of being inactive with very little energy. This period may last a few days or a few weeks.

A hamster's teeth are always growing. To make sure your hamster's teeth don't become overgrown, you should give it hard treats, such as branches from fruit trees, once a week.

Caring for Your Hamster

Like all pets, hamsters depend on their owners' care to stay happy and healthy. You'll need to set aside time each day to care for your pet. This means giving your hamster fresh food and water, cleaning its cage as often as necessary, and making sure it gets plenty of rest and exercise.

Hamsters are small animals and don't eat very much. You should give a pet hamster about 1 tablespoon (14.3 g) of **pellets** or seed mix once a day. You can also give it treats such as greens, a piece of cauliflower, a slice of apple, or a few raisins once a day.

pellets

Pet Report

You need to keep your hamster's cage clean so it doesn't become smelly and so your hamster doesn't get sick. Remove any waste you see every day. You should change your hamster's bedding every week.

If you give your hamster too much food or too many treats, it can become overweight.

Hamster Home

Your hamster's cage is its home. The type of cage you should get depends on what kind of hamster you have. However, bigger is always better. Most hamsters will use one corner of their cage for waste, another for food storage, and another for sleeping.

Hamster cages should be at least 360 square inches (2,318 sq cm) and have a solid—not wire—bottom. You should line the cage floor with at least three inches (7.6 cm) of bedding. The type of bedding you should use depends on the type of hamster you have.

Pet Report

You should never use pine or cedar wood shavings as hamster bedding. They are sharp and can cut your hamster and make it sick. Fluffy bedding can also be harmful to hamsters.

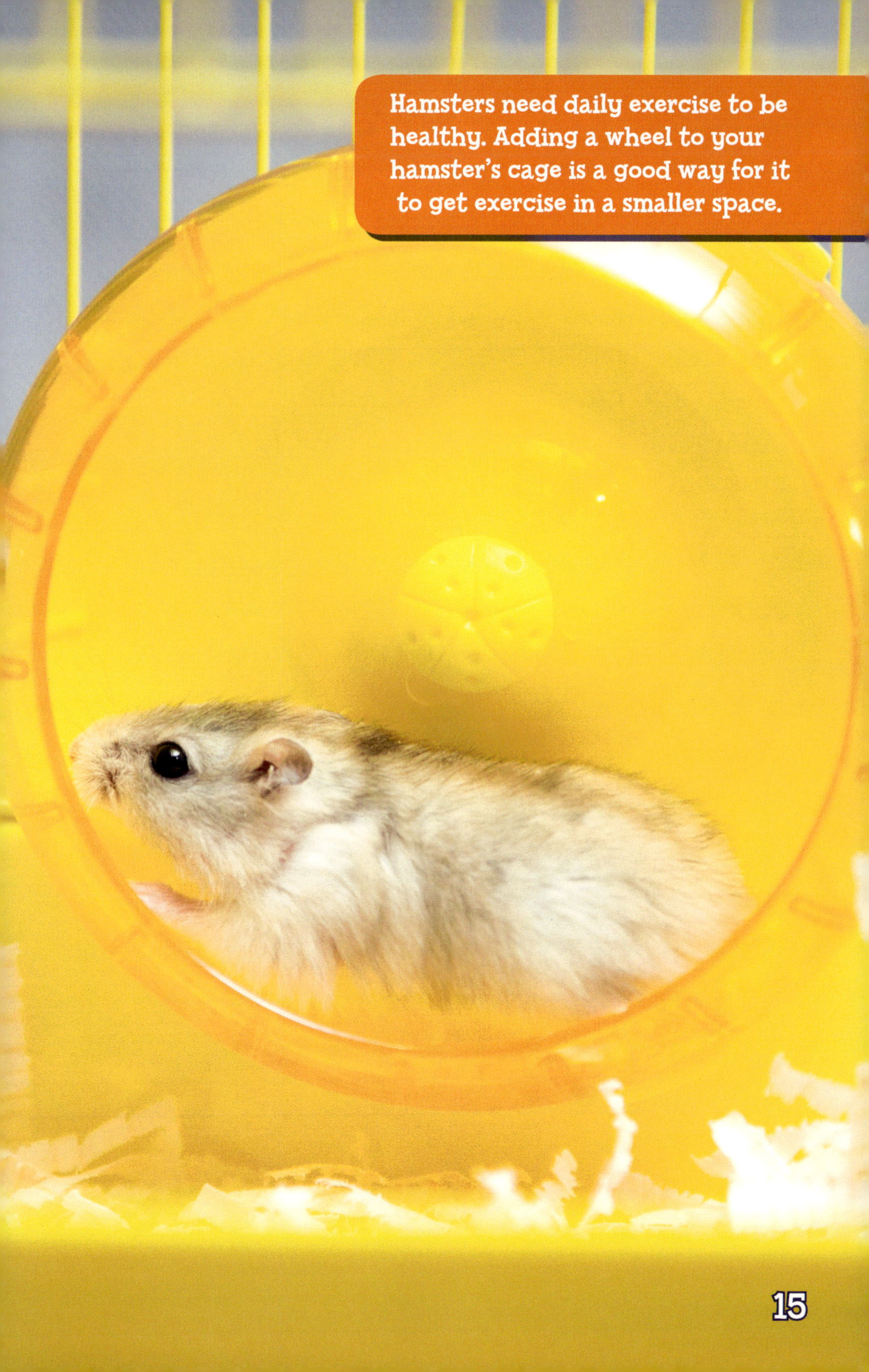

Hamsters need daily exercise to be healthy. Adding a wheel to your hamster's cage is a good way for it to get exercise in a smaller space.

On a Roll

Putting your hamster in an exercise ball is another good way for it to get exercise and explore. Hamster exercise balls are made of plastic and have air holes so your hamster can breathe. If you want your hamster to have time outside its cage, an exercise ball makes it possible in a safer way.

You should always keep a close eye on your hamster while it's in its ball. Don't let it run on hard floors because the ball will move too fast. You should only put your hamster in its ball once a day for about 20 minutes.

You should never let your hamster play in its ball with other pets in the room. Be sure your hamster stays away from stairs because it may fall and get hurt.

Grooming

Hamsters are very good at **grooming** themselves. They spend about 20 percent of their time grooming. If your hamster stops grooming, something is wrong.

Unless your hamster gets very dirty, you probably won't ever need to give it a bath. Water can take away special oils found on your hamster's coat. If your hamster is dirty, you can try brushing it with an unused toothbrush and a small amount of warm water. Don't use shampoo. Make sure your hamster is completely dry before putting it back in its cage. You can also give your hamster a dust bath.

Pet Report

Hamsters leave behind their scent to mark their **territory**. When hamsters groom themselves, they're removing the scent of their owner. They spread their scent from scent **glands** at the top of their hips.

Cleaning your hamster's cage regularly is a good way to keep your hamster from getting dirty and smelly.

A Happy Hamster

Even though hamsters are tiny animals, taking care of one is a big responsibility. They need a clean cage that's big enough, the right bedding, the right food, the right exercise wheel, and enough sleep and exercise. Remember to never put Syrian hamsters in the same cage. You should also never forcefully wake up your hamster during the day.

The better you take care of your hamster, the more likely that it will be happy and healthy. If you're willing to take all this on, a hamster might be a good pet for you.

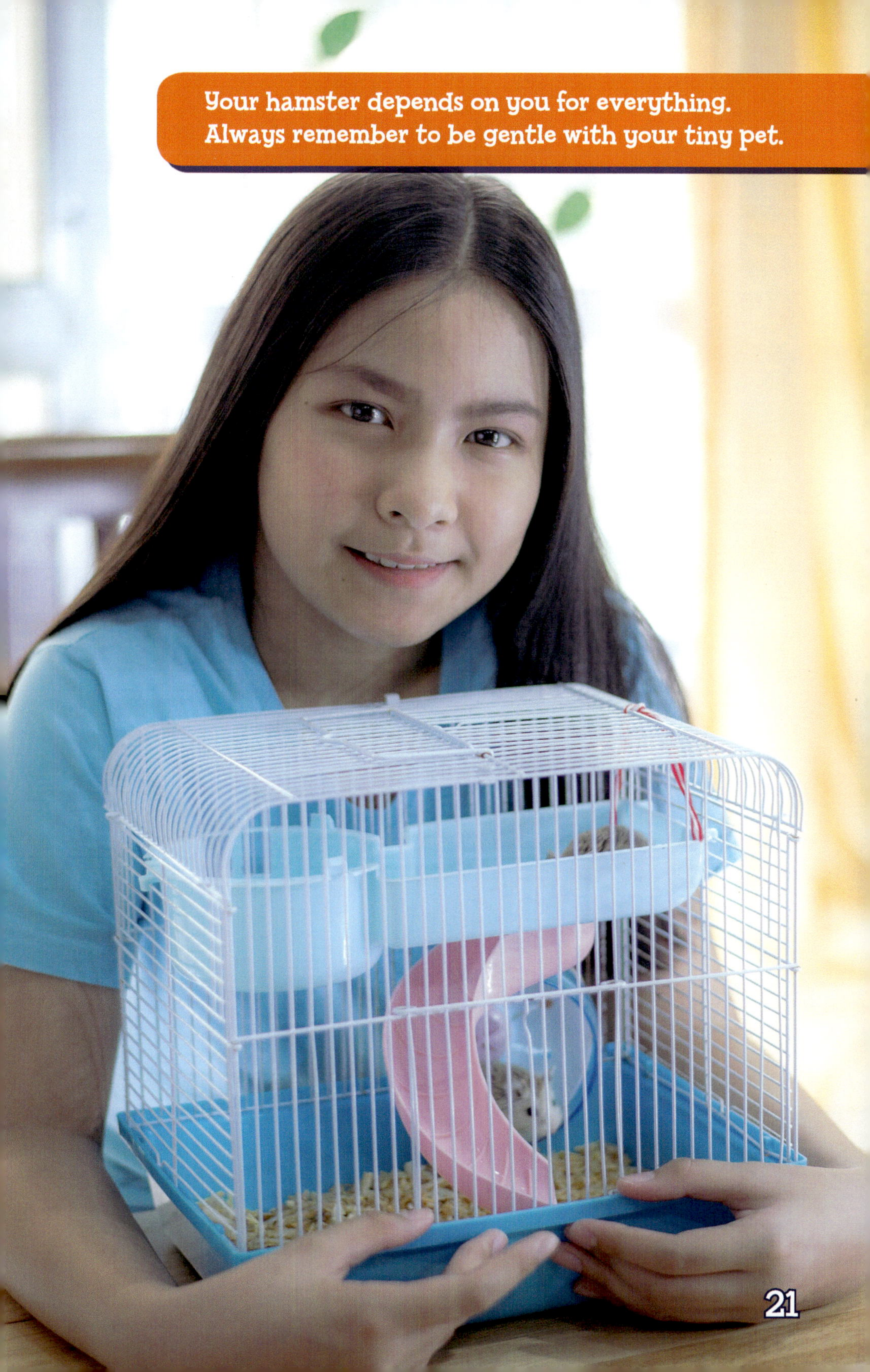

Your hamster depends on you for everything. Always remember to be gentle with your tiny pet.

What You'll Need

Syrian hamster:	$5 to $20
Cage:	$35 to $60 for a good cage
Bedding:	$11 for a 30-gallon (113 L) bag of aspen shavings or $20 for a 22-gallon (85 L) bag of paper-based bedding
Water bottle:	$5 for plastic or $7 for glass
Food dish:	$6 from a pet store
Food:	$3 to $10 depending on size and brand
Fruits and vegetables:	$10 for a variety of safe foods
Treats:	$2 to $9 depending on size and brand
Exercise wheel:	$8 to $10 depending on size
Exercise ball:	$3 to $5 depending on size
Hideout:	$5 to $8 depending on size and material
Toys:	$8 for a wooden bridge or $9 for plastic tunnels
Chew toys:	$2 to $5 each
Hamster carrier:	$9 to $11

Total estimated cost for beginning supplies:

$112 to $190

Glossary

burrow: A hole in the ground that an animal such as a hamster or fox makes to live in or for safety.

expedition: A journey for a particular purpose.

extinct: No longer existing.

fossil: Something, such as a leaf, skeleton, or footprint, that's from a plant or animal that lived in ancient times and that you can see in some rocks.

gland: A body part that produces something that helps with a bodily function.

groom: To clean and care for an animal.

hibernate: To pass all or part of the winter in an inactive state in which the body temperature drops and breathing slows.

pellet: A usually small, rounded piece of food.

responsibility: The quality or state of being in charge of someone or something.

rodent: A small, furry animal with large front teeth, such as a mouse or rat.

territory: An area that is occupied and defended by an animal or group of animals.

zoologist: A person who studies the branch of science that deals with the study of animals and animal behavior.

Index

Websites

Due to the changing nature of Internet links, PowerKids Press has developed an online list of websites related to the subject of this book. This site is updated regularly. Please use this link to access the list:
www.powerkidslinks.com/bpfm/hamster